60
S U P E R
S I M P L E
MAGIC TRICKS

By Shawn McMaster

Illustrated by Leo Abbett

Lowell  House
Juvenile
Los Angeles

CONTEMPORARY BOOKS
Chicago

For my daughter, Hannah, who made me a beginner all over again.

ACKNOWLEDGMENTS

Special thanks to David Jockisch for his contribution of one of the tricks in this work. Extra special thanks to Kathy and Terry Bergeron: two very special people who, without their help during a crucial time in my life (on top of all the other help they have offered in the past), this book may never have been finished.

Publisher: Jack Artenstein
Vice President, Juvenile Division: Elizabeth Amos
Director of Publishing Services: Rena Copperman
Managing Editor, Juvenile Division: Lindsey Hay
Editor in Chief: Amy Downing
Art Director: Lisa Theresa Lenthall
Cover photograph: Ann Bogart

Lowell House books can be purchased at special discounts when ordered in bulk for premiums and special sales. Contact Department JH at the following address:
Lowell House Juvenile
2029 Century Park East, Suite 3290
Los Angeles, CA 90067

Library of Congress Catalog Card Number: 96-390

ISBN: 1-56565-384-x

Manufactured in the United States of America

10 9 8 7 6 5 4 3

CONTENTS

THE WAND IN THE PURSE

From a small coin purse you remove a full-size magic wand! The wand is solid and too long to fit in the purse.

WHAT YOU'LL NEED

• small change purse (the kind with clamps that close at the top is best)   • pair of scissors
• magic wand, about 12 inches long   • long sleeves

GETTING READY

❶ Cut a small slit about 2½ inches long in the bottom of the purse.

❷ Put the tip of the wand into this slit. Push it up into the purse until it touches the top.

❸ Run the rest of the wand down your left sleeve. You can now hold the purse in a natural fashion without anyone suspecting anything. The wand is hidden in your sleeve and behind your hand as you hold the purse.

SHOWTIME!

❶ Allow your friends enough time to clearly see that all you are holding in your hand is a small change purse.

❷ Snap open the purse and pretend to root around inside as if you are looking for something.

❸ Exclaim, "Ah . . . here it is!" and pull out the wand through the mouth of the purse.

❹ Close up the purse and put it in your pocket. Tap the wand on the table a couple of times to prove it is solid. Then, continue with your other tricks, using your magic wand from time to time.

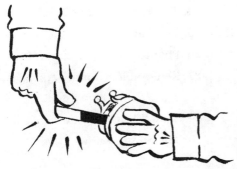

THE BLACK-BELT BILL

You demonstrate the magical strength of a dollar bill when you use it to break a regular wooden pencil in half.

WHAT YOU'LL NEED
• **dollar bill** • **thin #2 pencil, at least 7 to 8 inches long**

SHOWTIME!

❶ Let your friends examine the bill and the pencil.

❷ Tell one volunteer to hold the pencil at both ends so the middle portion is uncovered.

❸ Fold the bill down the center lengthwise from end to end. Hold it so it looks like a "V."

❹ As you hold the bill at the end with your fingers and thumb, insert your index finger into the fold of the bill.

❺ Raise the bill into the air and quickly bring it down onto the center of the pencil. Your index finger, hidden in the fold of the bill, will actually break the pencil.

❻ Unfold the bill and hand it out to your astonished audience to examine once again.

NOTE: The longer and thinner the pencil used, the better. Remember to aim for the center of the pencil and hit it as hard as you can without hurting your finger.

ARE YOU SURE?

A volunteer chooses one of three cards, seen by everyone. But, when the volunteer takes a second look, it is an entirely different card! In fact, the one the volunteer thought he or she was taking has completely vanished from the cards in your hand!

WHAT YOU'LL NEED
• **four different playing cards** • **pair of scissors** • **clear tape**

GETTING READY

❶ You must first construct a special card for this trick. To do this, take one of the cards and cut it in half diagonally from corner to corner with the scissors.

❷ With the clear tape affix one of the half pieces to the face of another card. You do this by creating a "hinge" out of a strip of tape. Fold the strip of tape in half, sticky side out, and attach it to the back of the cut piece and the face of the whole card so that the piece can "open" like a book.

❸ Now place another single card in between the flap piece and the whole card, lining it up perfectly with the flap's edges.

❹ Place the remaining single card on top of this entire set-up. It should slightly overlap the flap, hiding the other card underneath it. It should now appear that you are holding a fan of three cards in your hand. You need to cover the bottom of the cut card with your thumb. If all is lined up properly, there should be no sign of the hidden card underneath the flap.

SHOWTIME!

❶ Hold the three cards in a fan shape so that the faces can be seen. Tell a volunteer to remember the names of the three cards.

❷ Turn the cards face down and tell your volunteer to take out the middle one, without looking at the face. Your volunteer will be looking at the back of the secret hidden card, and that will be the one he or she removes from the fan. As soon as the card has been removed, slide the two cards remaining in your hand together slightly. This should hide the flap from view.

❸ Ask your volunteer which card he or she is holding. Your volunteer will name the card he or she remembers being in the center. Ask, "Are you sure?" Have your volunteer turn over the card and show it to the audience. They all will be amazed to see that it is an entirely different card! You can now turn over the "two remaining cards" in your hand to show that is all you have.

THE BALLOON
TUBE

A tube and balloon are shown. The balloon is blown up within the tube, its ends extending from either end of the tube.

You now push two sharpened pencils through the tube. Both pencils actually go through the tube and out the other side. The balloon, however, magically stays intact!

WHAT YOU'LL NEED

• empty cylindrical oatmeal container   • pair of scissors
• cardboard tube, approximately 2 inches long and 1 inch in diameter
• masking tape   • two sharpened pencils
• long balloon, big enough to fill the inside of the oatmeal container when inflated

GETTING READY

❶ First make the special tube needed for this trick. With the scissors, cut off the top and bottom of the oatmeal container.

❷ Attach the 2-inch cardboard tube horizontally to the inside of the oatmeal container. It must be completely hidden inside, and not protrude from either end of the container. Attach it by running a piece of masking tape through the 2-inch tube. The piece of tape must be long enough to extend out both ends of the tube. Press firmly on the tape so it sticks to the inside of the tube.

❸ Now place this whole thing inside the oatmeal container, an inch or two from the top. The tube should be straight up and down, securely attached to the inside of the oatmeal container. No one should know about this tube. It is the secret to the trick.

❹ With the pencils, punch four holes into the sides of the oatmeal container within the 2-inch-long vicinity of the cardboard tube. Push the pencils through at different angles from each other—going in one side and out the other—making two holes with each pencil. Remove the pencils. You should now have an oatmeal container with four holes punched into the sides, and a secret tube attached to the inside wall.

SHOWTIME!

❶ Display the oatmeal container. Push your hand through the container to show that it is empty. Of course, don't show the *inside* of it.

❷ Lower the balloon into the oatmeal container from above. Secretly let the balloon go through the cardboard tube.

❸ Blow up the balloon, allowing it to inflate through the cardboard tube. The top and bottom of the balloon will fill with air, while the middle will stay pinched inside the secret tube. The audience will assume the balloon fills the entire oatmeal container. Tie off the balloon.

❹ Now push the pencils through the holes you made earlier.

❺ Hold up the balloon and oatmeal container with the pencils in it. It will appear to your audience as if the pencils have somehow magically penetrated the balloon!

BIRDS OF A
FEATHER

The four kings, jacks, queens, and aces are separated—only to magically group them-
selves back together again. Birds of a feather do flock together!

WHAT YOU'LL NEED
• sixteen cards from a card deck: four kings, four jacks, four aces, and four queens

SHOWTIME!

❶ Display the four kings and deal them out face up on the table. Deal the first one up to the left. Deal the next one to the table about 3 inches to the right of the first card. The third one goes about 3 inches below the first card. The fourth goes 3 inches below the second card. If you dealt the cards out properly, they should form a square on the table.

❷ Now deal out the jacks in the same manner, putting one jack on top of each king.

❸ Do the same with the aces, and queens. When you have finished this, you should have four piles of cards in a square on the table. Each pile of cards should contain a king, jack, ace, and queen.

❹ Pick up each pile, without changing the order of any of the cards, stacking one on top of the other. You should now have a small stack of sixteen cards.

❺ Turn the stack face down and ask a friend to give the cards a single cut, anywhere he or she wants, and replace the cut. Your friend can do this over and over until satisfied.

❻ After your friend has finished cutting the cards, pick them up and deal them back out face down in exactly the same manner as before, creating four separate piles of cards.

❼ You should now have four face-down piles of four cards each. Turn over the piles to show that although the cards had been separated, all of them have gathered together again!

NOTE: At the end of the trick, the piles may be different with each performance. In other words, one time you may turn over the upper left hand pile to reveal the four kings, and another time that same pile may be the four aces.

6 THE COIN
IN THE ROLL

A borrowed coin magically appears in the center of a bread roll chosen from a basket of rolls.

WHAT YOU'LL NEED

• coin (borrowed, if possible) • basket of small dinner rolls • handkerchief

SHOWTIME!

❶ Ask someone to lend you a coin and remember the date on it. Also have someone choose a bread roll from the basket and hold onto it.

❷ Hold the coin in the fingertips of your left hand. Cover the coin with the handkerchief. Let a few friends feel it to prove it is still there.

❸ Reach over with your right hand and pretend to take the coin, through the handkerchief, in your right fingertips. However, you *really* allow the coin to fall into your left palm. Your right fingertips only grip the center of the handkerchief, *pretending* to hold the coin through the cloth. Move your right hand away from your left hand.

❹ Now with your left hand, grip a corner of the handkerchief. The coin is still hidden in this hand—hidden by your curled middle, ring, and pinkie fingers. But because your hand is now gripping the handkerchief with its index finger and thumb, it will look very natural. Whisk the handkerchief away from your right fingers. *The coin is gone!*

❺ Immediately take the roll from your other friend and hold it in your left palm (secretly hiding the coin from view at the same time).

❻ With your thumbs on top of the roll and your fingers underneath, break the roll open—pushing the coin up through the bottom. It will look like the coin was in the middle of the roll! And the date on the coin will prove it!

COLORFUL

CONJURING

With your psychic powers, you guess the color of your friend's secretly chosen crayon.

WHAT YOU'LL NEED
• **about ten crayons: make sure the colors are
completely different from one another**

SHOWTIME!

❶ Place the crayons on the table. Tell your friend to pick a crayon. Turn your back to the audience and cup your hands behind your back.

❷ When a choice has been made, have your friend place the crayon into your hands and hide the other crayons.

❸ Now, turn back to face your friend. As you instruct your friend to concentrate, secretly and quickly draw on the thumbnail of your left hand with the crayon behind your back. Just a couple of scribbles will do.

❹ As your friend concentrates, you pretend to think as well. Bring your left hand out from behind your back, making sure it is wide open so your friend can see you are not holding the crayon. Keep the back of your hand facing toward yourself so your friend doesn't see the fingernail. Dramatically place your left fingertips on your forehead as if you are reading your friend's mind. Keep your left thumb curled in slightly. As you bring your hand to your head, quickly glimpse the color that is drawn on your thumbnail.

❺ After you announce the color, bring the crayon out from behind your back with your right hand and give it to your friend. At the same time, drop your left hand to your side and rub the crayon off your nail with your left index finger.

13

THE CUP THROUGH THE TABLE

A cup magically passes through a solid table!

WHAT YOU'LL NEED

• table with flaps or tablecloth that hides your lap from audience   • quarter or half dollar
• small plastic drinking cup   • sheet of newspaper

SHOWTIME!

❶ Sit down to do this trick. Show the coin and state that you will make it magically pass through the table.

❷ Place the coin in the center of the table, then place the cup mouth down over the coin.

❸ Wrap the sheet of newspaper completely around the cup. The paper must be flat against the table and around the cup. Your friends will see that there is no way that you can get to the coin without them seeing it.

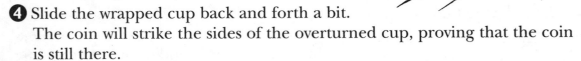

❹ Slide the wrapped cup back and forth a bit. The coin will strike the sides of the overturned cup, proving that the coin is still there.

❺ Strike the top of the cup and then lift up the wrapped cup, moving it back toward you until it is just past the edge of the table. Act very confused that the coin is still there and did not go through the table.

❻ Cover the coin again and repeat steps 4 and 5. Again the coin will still be there. Act even more frustrated.

❼ Repeat steps 4 and 5 one more time, but this time as you bring the wrapped cup back toward you, you secretly let the cup slip out of the newspaper into your lap. The newspaper will keep the shape of the cup. Keep your knees together, forming a lap for the cup to fall in.

8 Acting as if you are still holding the cup, place the newspaper shell back over the coin, continuing to hold it. Act as if you are upset that the trick has failed three times, and, in anger, you hit the top of the newspaper shell with your other hand, flattening the newspaper. At the same time, you open your knees and allow the cup to fall to the floor. The visual of the "cup" collapsing combined with the sound of the cup bouncing around under the table creates a perfect illusion.
It actually looks as if your cup was pushed right through the table.

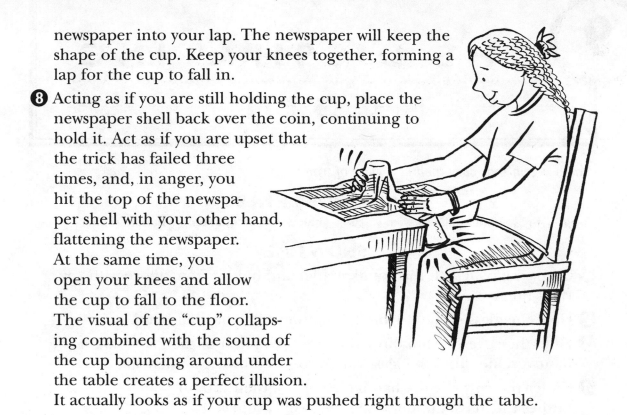

NOTE: Be sure that each time you lift the wrapped cup up to reveal the coin, you don't lift it too high. The edges of the newspaper should still lightly touch the table's surface. That way, when you finally allow the cup to fall into your lap, your audience won't see it go.

9 THE DISSIPATING COIN

Watch a coin magically melt in a glass of water.

WHAT YOU'LL NEED

• **glass filled halfway with water**   • **half dollar or quarter**   • **handkerchief**

SHOWTIME!

❶ Cover the coin with the handkerchief and hold it from above with your right fingers.

❷ Hold the glass of water from the bottom with your left hand.

❸ Hold the covered coin directly above the mouth of the glass. Lower the handkerchief until the glass cannot be seen by the audience.

❹ Under the cover of the handkerchief, your left thumb pushes the glass, tipping it slightly toward your left fingers. Your right hand drops the coin.

❺ The coin will bounce off the side of the glass and fall silently into your left palm. Your friends will hear the coin hitting the glass, and think the coin dropped into the water.

❻ Your right hand now grips the covered glass from above and sets it down on the table. The coin remains secretly hidden in your left hand. Tell your friends it takes a few moments for the coin to "completely dissolve," then whisk the handkerchief off the glass to show there is nothing in it but water! If you wish, drink the water.

CLINK!

WITH A GRAIN OF SALT

Find your buddy's chosen card in a very unusual manner.

WHAT YOU'LL NEED
• **several grains of salt**   • **deck of cards**

GETTING READY

Put the grains of salt on your index finger. They should stick to your finger. If not, wet your finger slightly to help the salt stick.

SHOWTIME!

❶ Ask a friend to shuffle the deck, spread out the cards, and choose one.

❷ After the card has been chosen, scoop up the rest of the cards and straighten the deck back up. Be careful not to bump the salt off your finger while doing this.

❸ Cut the deck in half, secretly brushing the salt off your finger with your thumb onto this portion of the deck as you do so. Ask your friend to replace his or her card back on top of this portion.

❹ Your friend will unknowingly place his or her card right onto the grains of salt. You can now replace the other half of the deck on top.

❺ Tell your friend that you are about to find the chosen card in a very unusual way. Place the deck in your friend's palm. Step to the side of your friend and give the elbow of his or her hand that is holding the deck a quick, sharp shove. (Not too hard! You don't want your friend to drop any of the cards.) At that moment, the deck will separate into two halves, where the salt is.

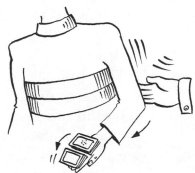

❻ Turn over the top portion of the deck to reveal your friend's card.

THE HOT CARD

You find your friend's chosen card in a deck—just by the "heat" it gives off.

WHAT YOU'LL NEED
• **deck of cards with a picture on the back**
(the picture on the cards must be able to be easily recognized as being
either right side up or upside down)

GETTING READY
Arrange all the cards so the pictures on the back face the same direction.

SHOWTIME!

1 Have a volunteer select a card. Turn your back and ask the volunteer to look at the card, then sandwich it between his or her two palms.

2 While your volunteer is carrying out your instructions, revolve the entire deck 180 degrees, keeping the cards face down the entire time.

3 Turn back around and spread the cards in a fan, and ask your volunteer to replace the card anywhere in the deck. You will find that most people will return the card exactly the way they pulled the card out. Therefore, the picture on the back of their chosen card will be in an opposite direction from the rest of the deck.

IF YOU NOTICE THE CARD IS GOING IN THE WRONG DIRECTION: Stop the volunteer to ask if he or she remembers the card selected. "Take one last look just to be sure you know what it is," you say, closing the fan of cards. Your volunteer will look at the card one last time. This is all the time you need. Revolve the deck 180 degrees *again*, spread the cards out again, and ask for the card to be returned. Either way, you should now have your volunteer's card in the deck facing a different direction than the rest of the cards.

4 You may now shuffle the cards, just as long as the top half gets shuffled back into the pack in the same direction as the other half.

5 Tell your volunteer, "Because you held onto one card longer than the rest, that one card should be hotter than the others." Go on to say that you will attempt to find the selected card by sense of touch. You will not even look at the faces.

6 Hold the deck up so your volunteer can see the faces as you begin spreading the cards. Act as if you are feeling the face of each card. What you are really doing is looking at the *backs* of the cards. Don't be obvious: just an occasional glance will do.

7 Act as if you are feeling each card for heat. When you come across the one with the picture going in the opposite direction, remove it from the deck and announce that *this* is the selected card.

THE HYPNOTIZED
BALLOON

You hypnotize a balloon and make it indestructible!

WHAT YOU'LL NEED
• **clear tape**   • **two inflated balloons**   • **three needles or straight pins**

GETTING READY

❶ Tear off three separate strips of clear tape, each about 1 inch in length. Apply all three pieces to one of the balloons in different places.

❷ Put both of the balloons on the table along with the needles. You are ready to go!

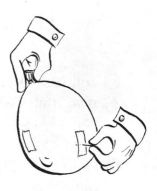

SHOW TIME!

❶ Hold up the first balloon, the one without tape. Stick a needle in it and watch it pop. (If it *doesn't,* you've got an even *better* trick on your hands!)

❷ Now pick up the taped balloon. Pretend to hypnotize it. Be as serious or as silly as you like. Snap your fingers and state that the balloon is now indestructible.

❸ Pick up a needle and stick it into the balloon through one of the pieces of tape. Stick the needle in only halfway, letting some of it stick out of the balloon. The balloon will not pop because the tape helps hold it together. Stick the other two needles partway through the other two taped areas on the balloon.

❹ Hold it up so everybody can see that the needles are, indeed, stuck into the balloon.

❺ Remove the needles. Snap your fingers again to remove the "trance" and stick the balloon with a needle again—this time in a spot not covered by tape. The balloon will pop!

KNOT A
PROBLEM

You challenge everybody watching to attempt to tie a knot in a piece of rope without letting go of either end. Everybody tries and fails ... until you show them how it's done.

WHAT YOU'LL NEED
• rope, approximately 4 ½ feet in length

SHOWTIME!

❶ Show your friends the piece of rope. Lay it out straight on the table and challenge any of them that care to try to tie a simple knot in the rope without letting go of either end. Tell them that they cannot even let go with one finger. They must grasp the ends in their fists and attempt to tie the knot without letting go in any way.

❷ Everyone who tries will fail. You take back the rope and show them how to do it.

❸ Lay the rope back out on the table in an upside-down "U" shape (like a horseshoe). This will make the ends easier to grasp.

❹ Cross your arms in front of your chest like a pretzel. With your arms still crossed, lean down and pick up the ends of the rope, one in each hand.

❺ Now slowly uncross your arms while holding onto the ends. Allow the rope to fall off your arms into a knot!

21

KNOTS FROM
KNOWHERE

Coil up a rope and drop it into a bag. After a snap of your fingers, you slowly pull the rope out of the bag, and your friends see that it has tied itself into several knots!

WHAT YOU'LL NEED
• rope, about 6 feet long   • empty paper bag

SHOWTIME!

❶ Have the bag open on your table. Pick up one end of the rope in your left hand, holding it in a fist. Your fist should be held knuckles down, fingers up.

❷ With your right hand, grip a bit of the rope next to your left hand. Your right hand needs to come up to the rope palm up and grip the rope in a fist. At this point both fists should look identical.

❸ Still holding the rope, turn your right hand completely over, thumb pointing down, making a loop. Open your left fingers just enough to grip this loop and hold it in place.

❹ Do this again, making another loop and holding it in place again with your left fingers.

❺ Continue looping the rope in this manner until all the rope has been coiled up and is being held in your left fingers. Let what's left of the rope dangle.

22

6 Drop the rope into the bag. But, as you do, push the dangling end back through the center of the coils with your right fingers next to the other end of the rope.

7 Snap your fingers over the bag.

8 Reach inside with one hand and grip the end of the rope that you pushed through the center of the coils. Continue to lift the end out of the bag, loosely closing the mouth of the bag around the rope as you do.

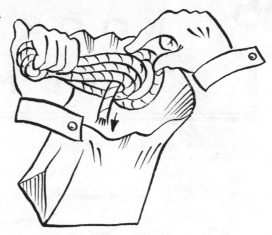

9 As the rope is pulled out of the bag, it will be tied in knots. The hand closing the bag around the rope will help keep the rope from bunching up and allow the knots to emerge smoothly.

10 Hand out the knotted rope and the bag for examination.

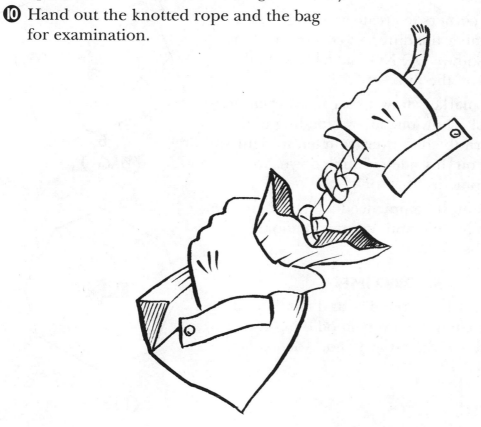

KOOKY KRAZY
KOMPASS

Two arrows drawn onto a cardboard "compass" magically point in all sorts of directions.

WHAT YOU'LL NEED
• pair of scissors   • stiff piece of cardboard   • black marker

GETTING READY

❶ With the scissors, cut out a piece of cardboard at least 2 to 3 inches square. This size can vary. Cut it to a size that can be comfortably held between your index finger and thumb.

❷ Trim the corners to create an octagon-shaped disk. Number the different corners in your mind as shown. DO NOT actually write the numbers on the disk.

❸ With the marker, draw an arrow on each side of the disk. Draw one arrow pointing to the right. Turn the disk over from left to right and draw an arrow on this side pointing down. You are now ready to practice this trick.

❹ This trick must be practiced a lot, so that your motions are fluid and natural. Memorize the trick for best effect!

SHOWTIME!

❶ Show your friends the disk and tell them it is a compass, but not a very good one. "It can never tell me which way to go," you explain.

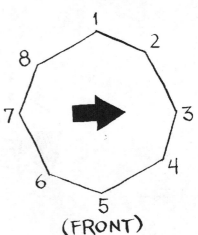

24

❷ Hold the disk in your left hand by placing your left index finger on corner **#4** and your left thumb on corner **#8** so the arrow is pointing to your left.

❸ With your right index finger pivot the disk around between your left finger and thumb. The arrows will point in the same direction. Pivot back to the first arrow.

❹ Say, "Oh, sure. It looks like it's working fine now, but give it a few minutes." As you are saying this, change the position of your left finger and thumb. Put your thumb on corner **#6** and your finger on corner **#2**.

❺ Flip the compass around once and the arrow will now point in the opposite direction. Flip the compass again to get back to the arrow pointing to the left.

❻ "See what I mean?" you exclaim. "It gets worse. Look!" As you say this, change your grip again. Now grip it with your thumb on corner **#7** and your finger on corner **#3**. Flipping the compass now will cause the arrow to point upward. Flip it back around to the first arrow.

❼ Change your grip one last time—this time your thumb on corner **#1** and your finger on corner **#5**. As you are doing this say, "With this compass I never know which way to go!" Pivoting the disk now causes the arrow to point down. Pivoting it back brings the arrow back to normal. Put the compass in your pocket saying you're glad you don't really have to use the compass or you'd be lost!

THE MAGIC NUMBER

You correctly predict a total that your volunteer arrives at after a brief series of math problems.

WHAT YOU'LL NEED

• pad of paper • pencil with eraser • envelope

GETTING READY

On a piece of paper from the pad write: "Your final total will be 1089." Fold the piece of paper in half and seal it in the envelope.

SHOWTIME!

❶ Hand the envelope to one person and the pad and pencil to another.

❷ Tell the volunteer with the pad to select a three-digit number. Tell this volunteer to make all three digits different.

❸ Now tell your volunteer to reverse the number and subtract the smaller number from the larger.

❹ When that is done, tell your volunteer to reverse *that* number and add the two together for a final total (see "Note" below).

❺ If your volunteer follows all your instructions exactly *and* does the math correctly, he or she will always arrive at the number 1089. It is just one of those quirks in mathematics that will *always* work.

❻ Now ask the person holding the envelope to open it and read the paper aloud. Take your bow!

NOTE: If a three-digit number is selected that causes the difference of the first subtraction problem to be 99 (or "099"), tell your volunteer to add a "0" on the end of 99 before adding.

MAGNETIC ATTRACTION

A pencil, pen, or magic wand clings to the palm of your hand without any visible means of support.

WHAT YOU'LL NEED
• **pencil or magic wand**

SHOWTIME!

❶ Grasp the middle of the pencil or wand with your left hand, putting your left thumb next to your index finger. The back of your fist should be facing your audience.

❷ Grasp your left wrist with your right hand. All the fingers of your right hand should wrap around the front of the wrist, while your index finger and thumb should be extended *behind* the wrist.

❸ Open your left fingers just enough to allow your right index finger to move up and press against the wand into your left palm. Now open your left hand and spread your fingers wide.

❹ From your audience's view, it will appear as if the wand is magically clinging to your left palm.

MAGNETIC ATTRACTION II

This is exactly the same trick as the last one, but it is done a bit differently. This version should only be done if your friends count the fingers on the hand holding the wrist and notice one missing. You can perform the trick again and still fool them.

WHAT YOU'LL NEED
• watch   • pencil   • another pencil or magic wand

GETTING READY
Slide one of the pencils into your watchband so that the pencil extends up your left wrist to about the center of your left palm. This pencil is hidden from view from the audience.

SHOWTIME!

❶ With your right hand, show the wand or other pencil to your friends. Keep the back of your left hand facing the audience while you do this to be sure they don't see the pencil in your watchband.

❷ Place the wand into your left palm, making a fist. It must be positioned between your left palm and the hidden pencil. The hidden pencil will keep it in place.

❸ Grasp your left wrist exactly as described in "Magnetic Attraction." Open your fist to show the wand floating.

❹ After displaying this for a few seconds, remove your right hand completely and show that the wand still clings to your palm.

❺ You can then remove the wand with your right hand so it can be examined. Some people may think there is something sticky on it. After it has been examined, you can replace it against your palm (and between the hidden pencil) and have it magically "cling" to your palm again.

> **NOTE:** If you are left-handed and wear your watch on your right wrist, all the above instructions can be reversed.

28

THE MAGIC LOOP

A loop of string magically passes through a friend's arm.

WHAT YOU'LL NEED
• piece of string or yarn, approximately 48 inches in length

GETTING READY

Tie the two ends of your string or yarn together in a knot to make one big loop.

SHOWTIME!

❶ Show the loop of string to your friend by hooking your thumbs through the loop and holding it between them.

❷ Ask your friend to extend his or her arm. With your thumbs still in the loop, lay the middle of the loop over your friend's arm and bring the ends down on either side.

❸ Now tell your friend that the loop is going to pass right through his or her arm. While you are saying this, try not to move the string much. Keep it and yourself still as you talk to your volunteer eye to eye.

❹ Once you know that you have your friend's attention, secretly hook your right index finger into the loop above your left thumb.

❺ Yell, "Now!" and very quickly, slide your right finger and left thumb away from each other, allowing the loop to come off of your right thumb at the same time. The loop will quickly unwrap around your volunteer's arm and end up underneath. However, it will look to your friend as if the loop actually went right through his or her arm!

❻ Right after this is done, quickly replace your right thumb into the loop, taking your right finger out at the same time. It will look as if nothing has changed, and the loop is just as it was before.

THE MIDAIR
PAPER CLIP
COLLISION

Two paper clips miraculously link in midair!

WHAT YOU'LL NEED
• **two paper clips** • **dollar bill**

SHOWTIME!

❶ Have the paper clips and bill inspected by an audience member. Then fold the bill into a "Z" shape.

❷ Clip this "Z" together with the two paper clips, exactly as shown in the illustration.

❸ Grip the ends of the bill in your hands and quickly pull them apart, snapping the bill open. The paper clips will fly off the bill into the air and link together! The clips actually link together just before they leave the bill, but it will look to your friends as if they linked while flying through the air.

TOP VIEW

FRONT VIEW

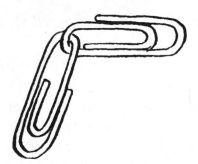

MATCHBOX
MAGIC

Matches disappear from their box with a wave of your hand!

WHAT YOU'LL NEED

• **two matchboxes (one empty and one slightly smaller matchbox filled with matches. This smaller one should be able to fit in the bigger empty box snugly without any gaps around the edges.)** • **pair of scissors**

GETTING READY

❶ Remove the drawer from the empty matchbox, and with the pair of scissors, cut off just the back wall of the drawer.

❷ Take the drawer from the smaller matchbox and cut a hole in the back wall big enough for your index finger to fit in.

❸ Place this smaller drawer into the bigger drawer so that they fit together flush. The hole in the drawer should be at the end where the back wall is missing on the larger drawer. Now slide both of these drawers together into the larger matchbox.

SHOWTIME!

❶ Hold the matchbox in your right hand. The hole should be toward the heel of your hand so as not to be seen by the audience.

❷ With your left hand, open both drawers at once about halfway, keeping them perfectly flush with one another. Show the matches.

❸ Close the drawers and wave your hand over the box.

❹ Open the drawer just as before, except this time, your right index finger slips into the hole in the back of the drawer to keep it in place. You now end up pulling out the outside drawer while the drawer with the matches is still in the box—safely hidden from view. It will appear as if all the matches just vanished into thin air!

31

WHAT ARE
....
THE CHANCES?

Remove three playing cards from a card box, lay them out face up on the table, and ask a friend to choose one. You then reveal a startling prediction you made before the performance that proves you knew which card would be chosen!

WHAT YOU'LL NEED

• adhesive label small enough to fit on the back of the coin • half dollar or quarter
• adhesive label small enough to fit on the back of the card
• three different playing cards (In this example, the three cards will be the
ace of clubs, the four of hearts and the seven of spades. *You* can use any three cards.)
• empty card box

GETTING READY

❶ On the label for the coin write the following sentence: "You will select the four of hearts." Stick this label on the back of the coin.

❷ On the label for the card write: "You will select the seven of spades." Stick this label on the back of the seven of spades card.

❸ On the inside of the flap of the card case write: "You will select the ace of clubs."

❹ Put the cards into the case and the coin in your pocket, and you are ready to go.

SHOWTIME!

❶ Remove the three cards from the case, being careful not to expose the label on the back of the card or the writing on the flap. Lay the cards on the table face up.

❷ Remove the coin from your pocket. Be careful not to expose the label on the back. Instruct a friend to select a card, and you will mark his or her choice with the coin.

❸ Place the coin (label side down) onto the chosen card. Remind your friend that he or she had an absolutely free choice.

❹ Whichever card is chosen, you reveal the appropriate prediction. For instance, in this example if the ace of clubs is chosen, you say, "Take a look at what I wrote on the flap of the card case before I came here." Then show your friends your prediction. If the four of hearts is chosen, tell your friend to turn over the coin and read the prediction. If the seven of spades is chosen, pick up the coin and tell your friend to turn over the card and read your prediction.

❺ Regardless of which card is chosen, you will prove you are right with a prediction, and your friends will think you are a real mind reader!

THE PAPER TREE

Create a very tall paper tree right before your friends' eyes from just a few sheets of newspaper!

WHAT YOU'LL NEED

• newspaper, at least three double sheets
(two newspaper pages that are connected)

SHOWTIME!

❶ Show your friends the sheets of newspaper. Open them out and begin rolling the first sheet into a tube from end to end. Start at the far right side of one page and roll across to the far left side. Try to keep the tube rolled as tightly as possible.

❷ When there are only a couple of inches left to be rolled, add the next sheet by overlapping the two ends of the pages by an inch or so. Continue to roll, rolling the second sheet into the tube.

❸ Take the third sheet and roll it in this same manner until you have a single newspaper tube.

❹ Make two long tears across from each other in one end of the tube, tearing the newspaper down just below the middle of the tube. Fold these torn halves down.

❺ Now insert your fingers into the center of the tube, right at the end of the tear you made, and pull the center of the tube upward from inside. The tube will extend into a long paper tree complete with leaves! Keep pulling upward until the tree reaches its full extent (you won't be able to pull it anymore). The first time you do this, you will be amazed how tall your tree will grow.

NOTE: The more pages of newspaper you use, the taller your tree will become. Just make sure the ceiling in the room is high enough for your tree!

THE PAPER LADDER

A few rolled up sheets of newspaper magically become a tall paper ladder!

WHAT YOU'LL NEED

• newspaper, two or three double sheets (the more sheets you use, the taller the ladder will be)   • clear tape   • pair of scissors

SHOWTIME!

1 Begin rolling the sheets of newspaper into a tube in the same manner as you did with "The Paper Tree" (page 34). However, the tube should be fairly loose.

2 Fasten the last sheet of newspaper with two small strips of tape—one on each end.

3 Now cut a section about 10 inches long and 1 inch wide out of the center of the tube.

4 Fold the ends of the tube backward, away from the torn out section, so that the newspaper tube now forms an upside-down "U" shape.

5 Insert your index and middle fingers into the ends from the torn side of the tube. Spread them apart, pressing your fingers against the insides of the ends.

6 Carefully shake your arms downward and the ladder will begin to drop toward the floor. Don't shake too hard or too long or the ladder may come apart and unravel.

7 Once the ladder has extended to a substantial height, stop shaking it and hold it up above your head for all to see!

THE PAPER
TUBE O' PLENTY

After showing your friends a normal piece of construction paper, you roll it into a tube and produce a handkerchief or scarf from inside!

WHAT YOU'LL NEED

• **stiff construction paper, 8½ by 11 inches** • **cardboard tube, approximately 5 inches long and 1 inch in diameter** • **masking tape** • **handkerchief**

GETTING READY

❶ Fold the construction paper in half, short end to short end.

❷ Attach the cardboard tube to the center of the construction paper close to the fold with two pieces of masking tape (one on each end of the tube).

❸ Once the tube is attached to the paper, stuff a handkerchief into the tube. Make sure it is packed in the tube with no corners sticking out.

❹ Now roll the construction paper, still folded in half, into a cylinder around the cardboard tube.

SHOWTIME!

❶ Hold the rolled-up construction paper tube upright in your left hand.

❷ Grip the ends of the construction paper, one in each hand, and pull the paper open all the way so that the cardboard tube is facing you. The audience will see a blank piece of paper.

❸ Bring your hands back together, allowing the construction paper to roll back into a loose tube. Don't accidentally reveal the hidden cardboard tube as you do this.

❹ Once the construction paper is rolled back up, turn it over end to end. (Be sure to practice this before you try it on a friend to be sure you know how to turn the tube over correctly. If you do it wrong, the cardboard tube will be seen and the trick will be ruined.) You must turn it over from left to right—NOT away from you.

❺ Once again, you are going to pull the paper open by pulling on the ends. When you do, you are actually showing your audience the same side of the paper. The cardboard tube will still be facing you. But because you turned the tube upside-down, your audience will think they are seeing the other side!

❻ Bring your hands back together again, allowing the construction paper to roll back into a loose tube.

❼ Now hold the tube in your left hand. Show your right hand to be empty and reach inside the tube and pull out the handkerchief. It will look like it magically appeared from nowhere!

PHANTOM
COINS

Your friends can hear coins clinking around inside your fist. How many? You ask someone to guess. Slowly open your hand to show you have ... none! There is absolutely nothing in your hand! Your friends must have heard phantom coins!

WHAT YOU'LL NEED
• **four or five assorted coins**

GETTING READY

❶ Put all the coins in your right palm.

❷ Loosely grip your left wrist with your right hand to let the coins jingle against your wrist, but not loose enough to allow them to fall out.

❸ Now close your left hand into a fist and shake it, still gripping the wrist with your right hand. The coins in your right hand will clink around, creating the illusion that there are coins in your closed left fist.

SHOWTIME!

❶ Shake your left fist (while gripping your wrist with your right hand and coins as explained in Getting Ready). Let your friends hear the coins.

❷ Ask someone how may coins he or she thinks you have. As you ask this, let go of your wrist with the right hand and then close it into a fist with your index finger extended. Point to the left fist with your right index finger as you ask your friend, "How many coins do I have in here?"

❸ After your friend guesses, open your left hand to show that it is empty. Your friends will be amazed! Keep the coins hidden in your right hand until you can secretly slip them into your pocket.

38

REMOVABLE
THUMB

Right before your friends' eyes, you create the illusion that you are actually pulling your thumb off of your hand.

GETTING READY

1 Hold your left hand in front of you, with your palm facing toward you.

2 Bend your left thumb tip down behind your palm.

3 Now hold your right hand, palm facing down, and lay it across the left fingertips. Your right thumb's knuckle should be touching your bent left thumb's knuckle.

4 Bend your right thumb tip down until it touches the side of your left index finger. Your two thumbs should now be touching one another knuckle to knuckle.

5 Now bend your right index finger down over the space where your two thumbs are touching. With your index finger in this position, your two thumbs should appear as one: your left thumb.

SHOWTIME!

1 Display your "left thumb" as already described in Getting Ready.

2 Now slide your right hand to the right slightly along your left index finger. Keep your right index finger in position the entire time.

3 If done properly, it will appear as if you have simply pulled the tip off of your left thumb! Try this in front of a mirror to experience this illusion yourself!

THE SPOOKY PENCIL

A pencil magically, and eerily, climbs out of a bottle all by itself!

WHAT YOU'LL NEED
• **black thread** • **thumbtack** • **pencil with eraser**
• **empty glass bottle, 10- to 12- ounce size**

GETTING READY

❶ Cut off a length of black thread about 21 inches long.

❷ Tie one end of the thread around the tip of the thumbtack. The other end you tie around your shirt button or belt buckle.

❸ Push the thumbtack into the eraser at the end of the pencil. You should now be holding a pencil with a length of thread on it. The other end is attached to you.

❹ Place the bottle on your table and hold the pencil by the eraser end, hiding the thumbtack. You are ready to perform.

SHOWTIME!

❶ Make sure your audience is at least 8 feet away from you before you begin. Show the pencil to your friends, holding it by the eraser end. Tell them it is haunted and that you will prove it.

❷ Pick up the bottle in your free hand and drop the pencil into the bottle, eraser end first. The thread will now extend from inside the bottle out to your button or buckle.

❸ Tell your friends to watch the pencil. After a few moments, slightly move the bottle away from your body. The pencil will appear to jump. Do this once or twice more. Then very slowly but steadily move the bottle away from your body. Because of the thread, the pencil will appear to climb straight up and out of the bottle. It can climb completely out and into your waiting free hand, if you like.

NOTE: It would be a good idea to wear a black or other dark colored shirt when doing this trick. The darker your clothes, the better the thread will be hidden from your audience. Be sure to practice this trick in front of a mirror so you can see just how little your arm has to move in order to get the pencil to move.

STATIC ELECTRIC STRAW

Using "static electricity" you cause a plastic straw to roll along the table. Whenever your friend tries to duplicate the stunt, he or she fails.

WHAT YOU'LL NEED

• 6-inch piece of drinking straw • 2-inch piece of drinking straw

SHOWTIME!

❶ Tell your friends you will show them how static electricity works. Show them the two pieces of straw and allow your friends to examine them.

❷ Place the small straw in front of you in a horizontal position.

❸ Rub the big straw through a friend's hair. This does nothing. It just makes your story believable.

❹ Hold the big straw upright on the side of the small straw opposite you. The bottom of the straw should touch the table. Position your head low to the table, as if you are trying to get a good look at the straws.

❺ When nothing happens, look a little confused. "Maybe I didn't get enough static," you say as you rub the big straw in your friend's hair again.

❻ Now position the big straw and lower your head exactly as before, but this time as you touch the big straw to the table, secretly give a quick little blow of air from your mouth toward the small straw. This will cause it to roll toward the big one. *At the same time,* move the big straw along the table away from you and the small straw. It will look as if the small straw is being drawn to the big straw by static electricity.

❼ Offer the two straws to your friend so he or she may try. Of course, it can't be done.

THE SWAMI KNOWS

Introduce your audience to a mind-reading swami. The swami successfully reads your mind and correctly names a random number chosen by the audience just moments before.

WHAT YOU'LL NEED
• friend willing to play the role of "swami"   • chair

SHOWTIME!

❶ Introduce your friend to the audience, then send him or her out of the room.

❷ Sit down in a chair that your friend can stand behind.

❸ Have your audience agree upon a number from one to ten.

❹ Have your swami friend come back in the room, stand behind you and place his or her hands lightly on your temples.

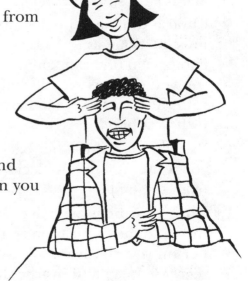

❺ At this moment you grit your teeth together the amount of times equal to the number chosen by the audience. Your friend will be able to feel your temples move when you do this. He or she just silently counts the amount of times your temples move, then announces the chosen number!

NOTE: This can also be done with colors or objects. The way to do this is for you and your friend to decide on a code. Each object or color used would have a certain number assigned to it.

43

A TOUCH
OF ESP

Together your friends decide on one card out of ten lying on the table. Using your ESP powers, you correctly name the chosen card every time.

WHAT YOU'LL NEED
• **ten cards from a deck (one of them *must* be the ten of hearts, the ten of clubs, the ten of diamonds, or the ten of spades)**
• **secret helper**

SHOWTIME!

❶ Deal out the ten cards onto the table. Lay them out in the same design as the spots are arranged on the ten card. See the illustration.

❷ Choose your secret helper, but this must be done as if it was a random choice. No one can know that the person you chose is actually helping out with the trick. Use your acting ability to its fullest here!

❸ Explain that while your back is turned, you want everyone to decide on a card from the table.

❹ Once a card has been decided upon, turn and face your friends. Look at the person you chose a moment ago (your secret helper) and instruct him or her to begin touching cards at random. "Each time you touch a card that is not the chosen one, try not to think of it,"

you tell your helper. "But once you touch the selected card, mentally tell me to stop."

❺ As your helper begins touching the cards, be watching for when he or she touches the ten spot card. Your secret helper has been told to touch the spot on the ten card that corresponds to the chosen card. See the illustration. This will secretly tell you which card was chosen. Of course you say "no" to this card, but as soon as your helper touches the chosen card, you dramatically tell him or her to stop.

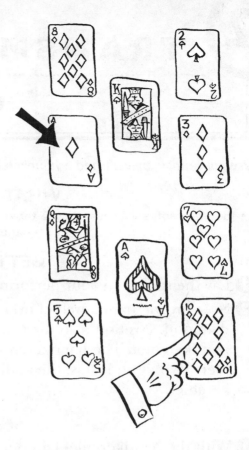

NOTE: Your secret helper must remember not to touch the chosen card until *after* he or she has touched the ten spot card—telling you which is the selected card.

If the card chosen by the audience is the ten card, your secret helper does everything exactly the same. He or she just touches the spot on the ten card that corresponds with the ten card. You, then, would immediately call out, "Stop!"

32 TRANSMOGRIFYING FORK

Use your magic powers and a handkerchief to transform a fork into a spoon!

WHAT YOU'LL NEED

• spoon • soft surface, such as a table with a tablecloth, a placemat, or a carpeted floor
• handkerchief • fork

GETTING READY

❶ Lay the spoon on your performing surface in a horizontal position.

❷ Now, lay the handkerchief over it with the handkerchief in the shape of a diamond. Position it so the spoon rests directly under the center of the handkerchief. The handkerchief should be rumpled a bit, not lying completely straight. If it is, the audience will see a tell-tale lump in the handkerchief.

SHOWTIME!

❶ With the handkerchief laid out (and the spoon secretly underneath) show your audience the fork.

❷ Lay it in the center of the handkerchief just in front of the hidden spoon (i.e., on the side away from you).

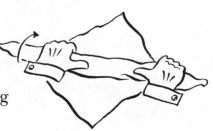

❸ Keeping everything on the table, begin to roll the fork up into the handkerchief. Start your roll from the *center* of the handkerchief, secretly picking up the spoon on your first roll and rolling it over the fork.

❹ Continue rolling the handkerchief into a long tube, bringing the top and bottom corners of the handkerchief toward one another. As the corners are about to touch, roll the handkerchief just a bit more, allowing the top corner to roll underneath the objects and the bottom corner to come to the top. This should not be done in an obvious manner. You've secretly turned the handkerchief over.

5 Stop at this point. Show your hands empty and snap your fingers over the cloth tube.

6 Now begin to pull the top and bottom corners away from each other, unrolling the handkerchief. Do this slowly so that the two utensils don't clink together. As you gently pull the two corners apart, this will slowly straighten out the handkerchief and dramatically reveal the spoon. To the audience, it looks as if the fork has changed into a spoon. Allow them to examine the spoon while you put away the handkerchief and its secretly hidden fork!

NOTE: This trick must be performed on a soft surface because when you are unrolling the handkerchief to show the change, the hidden fork will eventually have no place to go but on to the surface you are performing on. If that surface is a hard one, your audience will hear the hidden fork fall and will instantly know there is another utensil under the handkerchief.

AIRBORNE
PREDICTION

You offer to demonstrate your powers of ESP and write down the name of a card. You hand your friend a stack of cards, and, through a process of elimination, he or she ends up with one card—the one you predicted!

WHAT YOU'LL NEED
• **two identical cards**   • **glue or rubber cement**   • **twenty to thirty random cards from a deck**   • **pad of paper**   • **pencil**

GETTING READY

With the glue or rubber cement, glue the two identical cards together back to back. Make sure you glue them together so they are perfectly square. You now have one card with two matching faces! Put this special card in the middle of your stack of cards.

SHOWTIME!

❶ Show all the faces of the stack of cards. Your friends will see they are all different. Straighten the cards back into a stack and hand them to a volunteer.

❷ State you are going to make a prediction. With the pencil, write down the name of your special card on the pad. Put it aside, but in plain view. Don't let them see your prediction yet.

❸ Instruct your volunteer to toss the stack of cards into the air.

❹ As the cards hit the floor, eliminate all the cards that land face down. Scoop up all the faceup cards and hand the now smaller stack back to your volunteer to toss again.

❺ Because the special card has two faces, it will *always* land face up. Have the volunteer continue tossing until all of the cards are eliminated except one—the one whose name you wrote on the pad as a prediction!

48

THE CUT & RESTORED STRING

Show the audience your "magic protective straw" and run a piece of string through it. With a snip of your scissors, you cut the straw and string in half. Immediately you pull the string out to show it is unharmed!

WHAT YOU'LL NEED

• **straw**   • **string, 1 to 1½ inches longer than the straw**   • **pair of scissors**

GETTING READY

First, you must prepare the straw. Do this by cutting out a piece from the middle of the straw about ¾ inch long. This cut should not be too wide. You should be able to hold the straw with the uncut side facing the audience without them seeing anything strange.

SHOWTIME!

❶ Show your friends the string, then the straw. Hold the straw so the uncut side is facing them. The cut side should be facing you.

❷ Say, "If I were to cut this string the normal way, it would damage the string. But once I place it in this magic protective straw, watch what happens." Slide the string through the straw so it comes out the other end. If the end of the string is frayed, slightly moisten the end and twist it so it easily slides through and out the other side. Don't expose the cut-out portion of the straw while you do this.

❸ With the string inside, bend the straw in half at the cut-out portion. To cut the straw and string in half, insert the bottom blade of the scissors between the string and the straw in the cut-out area. When you cut, you will cut the straw in half, leaving the string totally unharmed.

❹ Slide the string out and let your friends look at it. It is still in one piece!

49

THE ELASTIC ARM

You create the illusion that you are actually stretching your arm right before your friends' eyes!

WHAT YOU'LL NEED
- **shirt with long, loose sleeves**

SHOWTIME!

❶ Put on the shirt with long, loose sleeves. Hold your arms out in front of you to show they are exactly the same length.

❷ Grasp your right wrist with your left hand—thumb on top, fingers on the bottom—and begin to pull in short little tugs.

❸ With each tug, shift your right shoulder and arm forward and away from you. This will pull your right sleeve up your arm little by little, creating the illusion that your arm is actually stretching!

❹ You can now hold your arms out in front of you again, but this time hold your right arm straighter and stiffer than your left. It will look as if it is now longer than your left arm by a few inches.

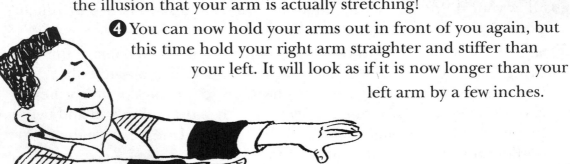

THE GHOSTLY HAND

Even though your two fingertips are touching your friend's closed eyelids, your friend feels a third ghostly hand tap on his or her shoulder. You two are the only ones in the room! (This trick can only be done with one person.)

SHOWTIME!

❶ Have your friend sit directly across from you.

❷ Point both of your index fingers at your friend's eye level.

❸ Move your fingers toward your friend's eyebrows and tell your friend to close his or her eyes.

❹ When your friend has done this, bring up the middle finger of your left hand forming a "V" with your two fingers. Place these two fingers gently on your friend's eyebrows—one on either side of his or her nose. Your right hand is now free to tap your friend's shoulder.

❺ Quickly tap, then bring your right hand back into its original position with the index finger pointing out. Curl up your left middle finger, leaving the left index finger pointing out. This is exactly the way your fingers were at the start of the trick.

❻ Immediately move away from your friend's eyes, allowing him or her to open their eyes. Your friend will see your two index fingers moving away, exactly as they were at the beginning of the trick. Watch your friend look around the room to see if someone else is there!

FOILED

AGAIN!

Display a few coins in the palm of your hand, and in a matter of seconds, one coin disappears! Where has it gone?

WHAT YOU'LL NEED

• **three or four silver-colored coins**   • **small piece of aluminum foil**   • **facial tissue**
• **pair of scissors**   • **handkerchief**

GETTING READY

1 Take one of the coins and lay the piece of aluminum foil over it.

2 Make an impression of the coin in the foil. Do this by rubbing hard on the foil with the tissue and the coin's image will appear. Rub it well to get every possible detail of the coin.

3 Then remove the coin from underneath the foil and cut out the foil coin with the scissors. You must do this very carefully so as not to bend the coin. Trim any edges that may need it. If all of the above steps are done properly, you will be left with a piece of foil that looks like a silver coin.

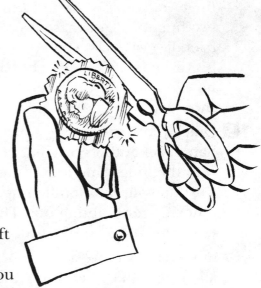

4 Place the foil coin on the palm of your left hand, and put the other coins around it, overlapping it a bit. It should look as if you just reached into your pocket and removed a handful of coins.

SHOWTIME!

❶ Display the coins in your palm and tell your friends to remember exactly how many you have.

❷ Cover your palm with the handkerchief. Then repeatedly close the hand with the coins into a fist, crumpling the foil coin into a ball. Your friends will only see your hand moving around under the cloth and hear the coins clinking.

❸ Once the foil coin is balled up, open your palm. With your right fingers, grip the ball of foil through the center of the handkerchief and whip the cloth off of your left hand, taking the ball with it.

❹ Toss the coins onto the table and allow everybody to examine them. While you are tossing the coins down, secretly drop the foil ball to the floor and put the handkerchief on the table for examination.

THE GYMNASTIC
DOLLAR BILL

With a few simple folds, you cause a dollar bill to turn completely upside down.

WHAT YOU'LL NEED
• dollar bill

SHOWTIME!

❶ Hold the bill right side up between your hands. The side with the president's portrait should face your audience.

❷ Begin by folding the top half of the bill down toward the audience.

❸ Next fold the right half of the bill away from you and to the left.

❹ Now unfold the half of the bill facing you (the original left half). Do this by moving this half back to your right with your right hand.

❺ Unfold the bill so the president's portrait is again facing the audience. It will now be upside down.

54

HOCUS-POCUS...
A PAIR!

Two decks of cards are shuffled. With just a snap of your fingers, you magically place two matching cards in exactly the same position in each deck!

WHAT YOU'LL NEED
• **two complete decks of cards**

SHOWTIME!

❶ Have your friend pick a deck of cards and shuffle it. You shuffle the second deck.

❷ Snap your fingers over both decks and announce that you have paired off two cards in each of your decks.

❸ Both of you begin to turn over cards in unison until each of you match. Believe it or not, this will happen *automatically*. Eventually two cards will match *exactly*—the same value and suit!

NOTE: This trick is not 100 percent accurate. However, the percentage of it working each time is very, very high. Try it by yourself a few times before you show it to anyone so that you can become comfortable with it.

THE HOPPING RUBBER BAND

A rubber band mysteriously hops from two fingers to the other two fingers of your hand all in the blink of an eye.

WHAT YOU'LL NEED

• one regular size rubber band
(the ones off a newspaper work well)

SHOWTIME!

❶ Let a friend examine the rubber band. Place the band around the index finger and middle finger of your hand, keeping your palm facing you.

❷ As you are pulling the band down over your fingers, pull the band down across the palm.

❸ Curl your fingers into a fist, with the tips of all four fingers going into the rubber band's loop. Let the band rest across your fingernails. To your friends it will look as if the band is going around just your index and middle fingers.

❹ Very quickly, open all of the fingers of your hand, keeping your fingers together.

❺ The rubber band will automatically jump from around your index and middle finger to around your ring finger and pinkie!

MAGICAL MATHEMATICS

You read your friend's mind and correctly name the number that he or she is thinking of at that very moment.

SHOWTIME!

① Select a volunteer and ask him or her to mentally select a number between one and ten.

② When your friend has a number in mind, instruct him or her to double it (example: if your friend thought of the number three, doubling it would make it six). Instruct your friend to keep all numbers in his or her head. He or she should not say anything out loud.

③ As soon as your friend has doubled the number, you tell him or her a certain number to add to it. This number can be *any* even number. *You* must remember this number (example: "add eight"; friend gets fourteen).

④ Once your friend has finished this math, tell him or her to divide the current number by two (friend gets seven).

⑤ Next, tell your friend to subtract the number that he or she originally started with for a final total (friend gets four). Tell your friend to concentrate on that total.

⑥ You now act as if you are reading your friend's thoughts, then call out the total. The total he or she is thinking of is also *half the number you had your friend add in step 3*. If your friend followed your instructions properly and did all the math correctly, his or her final total will always be half of the number you secretly remembered.

NOTE: Remember, you can have your friend add *any even number* you want. The final total will always be half of the number you give to add in Step 3.

AN INITIAL GUESS

Your friends jot down the initials of a boy they know on a square of paper you have given them. Another friend writes the initials of a girl he or she knows. All the squares are shaken up in a bag, and, with your ESP powers, you are able to remove the only square with the girl's initials on it.

WHAT YOU'LL NEED
• **sheet of paper**   • **pens or pencils**   • **paper bag**

GETTING READY
Tear, *don't cut,* the piece of paper into nine equal squares.
First tear the paper from top to bottom into three equal strips.
Then tear each of these strips into three equal squares. You will now have
nine squares torn from one piece of paper. Each of these squares will have *at
least* one ragged edge where it was torn. Some will have two or three. Only *one*
torn square will have ragged edges on all four sides.

SHOWTIME!

❶ Pass out the squares and pencils to your friends. If less than nine people
are present, give out more than one slip of paper per person. However,
the friend who gets the one with all four ragged edges shouldn't be given
more than one piece of paper.

❷ Tell your friends to write down the initials of a boy they know. Tell the
person with the square with the four ragged edges to write the initials of a
girl he or she knows. Of course, your back should be turned while all this
writing is being done.

❸ When all the squares are written on and put into a bag, mix
them and reach inside. Feel the edges of each square until you
feel the one with torn edges on all four sides. This is the one
you pull out . . . much to everyone's amazement!

THE PRE-SLICED

BANANA

You magically slice a banana into four separate pieces while it is still inside the peel.

WHAT YOU'LL NEED

• banana   • needle

GETTING READY

❶ Carefully stick the needle into the back of the banana, piercing the skin. Stick it all the way in until just before it pierces the skin on the opposite side. DO NOT LET IT COME OUT THE OTHER SIDE.

❷ Work the needle around from left to right a couple of times without piercing any other part of the skin. This will slice the fruit while still inside the peel.

❸ Do this two more times, spacing the slices out evenly. When you are done, you will have a banana sliced into four equal pieces, with only three tiny needle holes in the peel.

SHOWTIME!

❶ Show the unpeeled banana and offer to share it with three of your friends. Make sure your friends see that it is a whole banana and has not been peeled. They will believe it has not been tampered with.

❷ Wave your hand over the banana and begin to peel it. Watch your friends' amazement when they see the banana is already sliced! Give them each a piece and let them try to guess how you did the trick!

59

MYSTERIOUS RETURNING CARDS

You show the faces of two cards and place them in the middle of the deck. With a snap of your fingers and a toss of the deck, the cards magically return to your hand.

WHAT YOU'LL NEED
• deck of cards

GETTING READY

❶ Go through the deck and remove the eight and nine of clubs and the eight and nine of spades.

❷ Put the eight of clubs and the nine of spades aside. You will use them later. Put the eight of spades on top of the deck and the nine of clubs on the bottom.

SHOWTIME!

❶ Show your audience the faces of the eight of clubs and the nine of spades. Do *not* say the names of these cards! You should not draw special attention to them. Instead, just casually and briefly display the two cards.

❷ Bury each of them in different parts of the deck.

❸ Now, with your left hand, grip the deck face down with your thumb on top and fingers on the bottom.

❹ Snap the fingers of your right hand, and at the same time, jerk your left hand quickly and sharply to the right. When you do this, you should loosen your grip on the cards just enough to allow the deck to flow out from between the top and bottom cards into your waiting right hand. You will now be holding two facedown cards, the eight of spades and the nine of clubs, in your left hand. (It may take some practice to get this move right.)

5 Display the faces of *these* two cards and say, "The cards have mysteriously returned!" Even though these are not the same cards you originally showed, your audience should not catch on because you never said their names and didn't show them the faces for very long. The cards' designs are so similar that no one will suspect anything tricky!

NOTE: As with most magic tricks, this one should not be repeated. Your friends are likely to discover how the trick works if they see it again.

⑮ NOW YOU SEE IT—
NOW YOU DON'T

You make a coin disappear, then reappear right before your friends' eyes.

WHAT YOU'LL NEED

• **pair of scissors** • **paper cup** • **two sheets of matching colored construction paper** • **pencil** • **glue** • **coin**

GETTING READY

❶ Carefully cut out the bottom of the paper cup and discard it.

❷ Place the mouth of the cup down on one of the sheets of construction paper and trace around it with the pencil. Cut out the disc.

❸ Now glue the disc to the mouth of the paper cup. Carefully trim away any edges that need it.

SHOWTIME!

❶ Pick up the coin and show it to your audience.

❷ Place the coin on the second sheet of construction paper. Put the cup over it so the paper disc covers the coin. Be careful not to let them see the piece of paper glued to the cup as you cover the coin.

❸ Snap your fingers and invite someone to look into the cup. Your volunteer will look through the bottom and see the disc of construction paper. Because it matches the paper under the cup, it will appear as if the coin vanished into thin air!

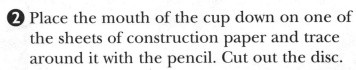

❹ Snap your fingers again and lift the cup to make the coin "reappear."

PICK AN OBJECT,
ANY OBJECT

You read the minds of everyone in the room to pick out an object the audience is concentrating on.

WHAT YOU'LL NEED
• **four random objects**   • **secret helper**

GETTING READY

❶ Lay the objects in a straight line on a table. Looking at them from left to right, the object on the extreme left will count as object 1. The next one will be considered object 2, the next object 3, and the one on the extreme right is object 4.

❷ Your secret helper will let you know which object is chosen by the way he or she sits.

The code is as follows:

A If object one is picked, your friend sits with his or her hands off to one side.

B If object two is chosen, your friend sits with his or her hands folded directly in front of him or her.

C If object three is chosen, your secret helper sits with his or her hands unfolded.

D If object four is selected, your helper sits with his or her arms folded at chest level.

SHOWTIME!

❶ Lay the four objects on a table in front of your audience. You tell them that you are going to leave the room and while you are gone, they will have to decide on one of these objects.

❷ After they have done so, you are called back into the room. As you enter the room, take a quick glance at the way your secret helper is holding his or her hands. Pretend to concentrate and act as if you are picking up their thought waves. Then proudly announce which item was chosen.

PREDICT-A-TOTAL

A sealed prediction that you made earlier in the day matches the total of four randomly selected three-digit numbers.

WHAT YOU'LL NEED

• pad of paper   • pencil   • sheet of paper   • envelope   • calculator (optional)

GETTING READY

❶ Flip back a few sheets of the pad. On this blank sheet write down four three-digit numbers. All of them must be written differently, as if they were all written by four different people.

❷ Total these numbers together either in your head or on a calculator. DO NOT do the math on the sheet where you have written the four different numbers.

❸ Whatever total you come to, write it on the separate piece of paper and seal it in the envelope.

❹ Now fold one blank sheet down over the sheet with the numbers and you are ready to go!

SHOWTIME!

❶ Hand your prediction to someone in the audience to hold. Tell them, "In this envelope is a piece of paper. On the paper I have written a number. The number is a prediction for later."

❷ Approach one volunteer and have him or her write a three-digit number on the pad. Hold the pad while the number is being written.

❸ Approach three more volunteers with the same instructions.

4 After all the numbers have been written underneath each other in a single column, you go to a fifth volunteer to total them. But, as you turn to walk to this person, you secretly turn the page to the sheet you prepared earlier.

5 This is the page the totaler will see. He or she will think these numbers were written by the other volunteers. He or she will do the math (make a calculator available if possible) and come to the same total you did before the trick began. Be sure to hold the pad yourself while this is being done. That way, your volunteer won't accidentally see the other page of numbers.

6 Have your totaler announce the total. Have your friend open up the prediction to show they match. Take your bow for this incredible display of psychic power!

A QUESTION OF STRENGTH

You magically remove all the strength from your friend's body so that he or she can't even move his or her fingers!

SHOWTIME!

1 Ask a friend to place his or her fingertips together and then bend the middle fingers down at the second knuckle.

2 Offer to put your friend through a series of simple tests. Ask your friend to pull his or her index fingers apart without separating any of the other fingers. Your friend will do this with no problem.

3 Next, have your friend pull the little fingers apart, again without separating any of the other fingers. Again, your friend will be able to do so.

4 Now the thumbs are put through the same test. Your friend will accomplish this also.

5 Say, "I am now going to take all your strength away." You now snap your fingers, "taking away" your friend's strength. Ask your friend to pull the ring fingers away from each other without separating any of the other fingers in the process. *Your friend will not be able to do it!*

NOTE: It is very important that your volunteer follows your directions exactly for this trick to work.

THE RUBBER
PENCIL

A wooden pencil held at your fingertips actually begins to bend as if it were made of rubber.

WHAT YOU'LL NEED
• **wooden pencil**

SHOWTIME!

❶ To create this optical illusion, hold the pencil at the eraser end between your thumb and index finger of your right hand. The pencil should extend away from your hand to the left. The grip of your thumb and index finger should be somewhat light.

❷ Begin to quickly move your hand up and down, allowing the pencil to bounce between your finger and thumb. Ask your friends to look at the pencil. If your grip on the pencil is correct, it will look as if the pencil is wobbling up and down with a rubbery quality about it.

❸ Pass the pencil around so everybody can see it is indeed made of wood.

A COIN...POOF! GONE!

A coin vanishes right at your fingertips!

WHAT YOU'LL NEED
• coin

SHOWTIME!

❶ You must be sitting down to perform this trick. Put the coin on the table in front of you for all to see.

❷ With your hand, reach out and slide the coin back to the edge of the table as if you were going to pick it up. When your hand reaches the edge of the table, allow the coin to secretly fall into your lap, but at the same time, bring your hand upward as if it were holding the coin. The back of your hand should be facing the audience.

❸ Tell your friends to watch carefully. Wait a second or so, then quickly wiggle your fingers and spread them wide. Show both of your hands empty. The coin has vanished!

R U B   I T
O U T

A quarter or half dollar is rubbed against your elbow and vanishes!

WHAT YOU'LL NEED
• **quarter or half dollar**

SHOWTIME!

❶ Show everybody the coin. The coin can be examined by any skeptics.

❷ Hold the coin in your right hand and tell the audience you will rub the coin into nothingness. Place your left hand on the back of your neck and put the coin against your left elbow.

❸ Begin rubbing the coin rapidly with your right hand. After a few moments, "accidentally" drop the coin onto the table. This should not be a big deal. It should look, and you should act, as if you really dropped the coin by accident.

❹ Pick up the coin in your left hand and pretend to transfer it to your right. Instead, secretly retain the coin in your left hand. Both hands now assume their original positions with the right hand rubbing the left elbow as if it contained the coin. Keep your fingers together while you rub. At the same time, drop the coin down the back of your shirt with your left hand. Make sure your shirt is tucked in!

❺ Slowly stop rubbing your elbow and at the same time spread your right fingers wide to show the coin has vanished. Show both hands to be completely empty.

69

A SPARE FINGER

Imagine the look on your friend's face when you open the lid of a box and display a real human finger!

WHAT YOU'LL NEED

• **box, approximately 4 by 2½ inches**   • **cotton batting**   • **pair of scissors**

GETTING READY

❶ Line the bottom of a small cardboard box with cotton batting.

❷ Cut a hole in the bottom of the box just big enough to insert one of your middle fingers. Push the finger up all the way through the hole and through the cotton. Hold the box in the palm of one hand and bend your middle finger down so it now rests on the bottom of the box. Rearrange the cotton around your finger to hide the hole. It should now appear as if your box contains a disembodied finger.

❸ Put the lid on the box and approach a friend.

SHOWTIME!

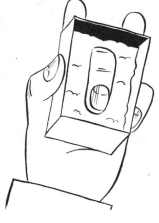

❶ Let your friend see the box in your hand and tell him or her that you carry a spare finger in it.

❷ Ask your friend to remove the lid, then watch for a reaction.

NOTE: For an added shock, once the lid is removed, let your friend stare at the finger for a few seconds. Then suddenly wiggle your finger and watch your friend jump!

A STICKY CHALLENGE

You stick a coin to your forehead, then wrinkle your brow until it falls. You now challenge a friend to do the same. Of course, your friend can't.

WHAT YOU'LL NEED
• wet sponge or cup of water   • coin

GETTING READY
Before the trick begins, *secretly* get your finger slightly wet by pressing it on a damp sponge or dipping it in a cup of water.

SHOWTIME!

❶ Press the coin to your forehead. Because of your skin's natural oils, it will stay there. Wrinkle your forehead until the coin falls. Challenge a friend to do the same.

❷ Once you have a volunteer, secretly rub your wet finger across the surface of the coin.

❸ Firmly press the wet side of the coin against his or her forehead, then move your hand away, taking the coin in your hand. Do not let your volunteer notice this.

❹ Because of the wetness left on the forehead by the coin, your volunteer will think the coin is still there. He or she will try and try to wrinkle his or her forehead to get the coin to fall, but will continue to feel the "coin."

❺ Your other friends will have fun watching your volunteer trying to get the coin to fall. If you wish, share the secret with your volunteer.

TAKE A NUMBER!

You lay out six cards in front of your friend. Each card has thirty-two different random numbers on it. Your friend mentally selects a number and picks up all the cards that contain that number. You correctly name the chosen number.

WHAT YOU'LL NEED
• six index cards • ruler • pen

GETTING READY

❶ Using the pen and ruler, draw lines across the index cards to divide each card into thirty-two equal squares.

Card #1

1	3	5	7
9	11	13	15
17	19	21	23
25	27	29	31
33	35	37	39
41	43	45	47
49	51	53	55
57	59	61	63

Card #2

2	3	6	7
10	11	14	15
18	19	22	23
26	27	30	31
34	35	38	39
42	43	46	47
50	51	54	55
58	59	62	63

Card #3

4	5	6	7
12	13	14	15
20	21	22	23
28	29	30	31
36	37	38	39
44	45	46	47
52	53	54	55
60	61	62	63

② Write a number in each one of these squares. Look at the cards at the bottom of pages 72 and 73 and copy the numbers exactly. This trick will not work with just any numbers.

SHOWTIME!

❶ Lay out the six cards on the table so your friend can see them all.

❷ Tell your friend to look them over. "Think of one of the numbers you see on these cards," you instruct your friend.

❸ Tell your friend to then pick up each card that has that particular number on it.

❹ When your friend finishes this, look at the number in the upper left-hand corner of each of the cards he or she picked up. If you now add those numbers together in your head, the total will be the number your friend thought of. Pretend you are trying to read the mind of your friend then announce this number as the one he or she selected. Watch the response you get!

Card #4

8	9	10	11
12	13	14	15
24	25	26	27
28	29	30	31
40	41	42	43
44	45	46	47
56	57	58	59
60	61	62	63

Card #5

16	17	18	19
20	21	22	23
24	25	26	27
28	29	30	31
48	49	50	51
52	53	54	55
56	57	58	59
60	61	62	63

Card #6

32	33	34	35
36	37	38	39
40	41	42	43
44	45	46	47
48	49	50	51
52	53	54	55
56	57	58	59
60	61	62	63

NOTE: This trick *can* be repeated with a different number selected, and you will be correct every time!

TOPSY TURVY
ACE

You cause the ace of diamonds to magically turn into the ace of hearts.

WHAT YOU'LL NEED
• three cards: ace of clubs,
ace of hearts, ace of spades

GETTING READY
Arrange the three aces in a fan as shown. The ace of hearts is placed upside down in the center and behind the other two aces. This creates the clever optical illusion that the middle card is the ace of diamonds.

SHOWTIME!

1 Show the three aces calling them the ace of clubs, ace of diamonds, and the ace of spades.

2 Turn the fan of cards face down and ask a volunteer to choose the ace of diamonds.

3 Of course, your volunteer will select the center ace and be surprised to see that it has "changed" into the ace of hearts.

4 You can now turn over the other two cards to show that there is no ace of diamonds.

UNDERCOVER COIN

You show your friends a coin and a handkerchief. Cover the coin and allow a few spectators to reach underneath the handkerchief to verify the coin is still there. When everyone is satisfied, you wave your hand over the cloth and the coin vanishes!

WHAT YOU'LL NEED

• **coin**   • **handkerchief**   • **secret helper**

SHOWTIME!

❶ Display both the coin and handkerchief. They both can be examined.

❷ Cover the coin with the handkerchief and grip the coin through it.

❸ You now offer to let a few spectators feel the coin. Each of them will reach under the cloth and feel the coin. Your secret helper is the last one you let feel the coin. When your secret helper reaches underneath to feel the coin, he or she actually *takes* the coin. Your secret helper "agrees" the coin is still there and removes his or her hand, secretly hiding the coin. This will have to be practiced a bit between you two until it looks natural.

❹ Now, wave your hand and toss the handkerchief into the air. The coin is gone!

NOTE: If you would like to add a bit more mystery to this trick, hide a coin identical to the one you are using somewhere in the room. After the coin has "vanished," tell someone to retrieve the coin you hid saying this is where the coin "disappeared to."

THE UNBREAKABLE
TOOTHPICK

You fold an ordinary wooden toothpick into a handkerchief. Through the folds, you snap the toothpick in half. Your audience hears it break. Yet, as you unfold the hanky, they see that the toothpick is still in one piece!

WHAT YOU'LL NEED

• **two wooden toothpicks** • **handkerchief with a hem sewn around all four sides**
(the hem on this type of handkerchief usually has an open end at one corner)

GETTING READY

Before the trick begins, secretly slide one of the toothpicks into the open end of the hem on the handkerchief. Don't forget which side the toothpick is on.

SHOW TIME!

❶ Lay the handkerchief out on a table in a diamond shape. The side with the hidden toothpick should be on your upper left-hand side.

❷ Place the other toothpick into the center of the handkerchief. The handkerchief should be folded into a square in the following manner:

A Bring the top corner down past the center.
B Fold the bottom corner up, overlapping the first corner.
C Now bring the side corners into the center one at a time.
D You should now have a square shape in front of you. The hidden toothpick will now be lying just to the left of the second one.

❸ Pick up this folded packet and feel for the hidden toothpick. Say, "I will now break the toothpick!" Break the hidden toothpick so everybody can hear it.

❹ Place the folded handkerchief back on the table. Wave your hand over it mysteriously, and say, "Abracadabra . . . mend yourself!" Unwrap the handkerchief and show the toothpick in one piece.

U P I N
A R M S

You "hypnotize" one of your friends and cause your friend's arms to float up in the air beyond his or her control.

SHOWTIME!

❶ Select a volunteer and tell him or her, "I will place you into a hypnotic trance." Wave your hand in front of your volunteer's face and snap your fingers. "You are now in a trance," you say. Have your volunteer step into an open doorway and press the backs of his or her hands against the sides of the door frame as hard as possible, imagining that each arm weighs two tons.

❷ While your volunteer is imagining, have your volunteer continue pressing his or her hands against the frame for approximately forty-five seconds. You can do this by secretly keeping an eye on your watch or clock, or you can just count to forty-five in your head. Instruct your volunteer not to stop pressing and imagining until you tell him or her to do so.

❸ At forty-five, you tell your volunteer to step forward and imagine his or her arms as being light as a feather. Because your volunteer isn't pressing anymore and the arm muscles are relaxing, your volunteer's arms will automatically rise into the air, seemingly beyond his or her control!

❹ Don't forget to snap your fingers again to take your volunteer out of his or her "hypnotic trance!"

THE FOUR
SNEAKY THIEVES

You tell your friends a story about a bank robbery and show the four jacks. "These are the four sneaky thieves," you say as you place them throughout the deck of cards. With a snap of your fingers, they all end up on top!

WHAT YOU'LL NEED
• **deck of cards**

GETTING READY

❶ Pull the four jacks from the deck, as well as any three extra cards.

❷ Take one jack and place the three extra cards behind this jack. Keep all these cards as straight as possible, hiding the extras behind the jack as best you can. These four cards should appear as one.

❸ Put the other jacks in a fan, face up on top of this first jack. You should now be holding a fan of four jacks in your hand, the last jack secretly hiding the three extra cards behind it. Close up the rest of the deck and put it face down on the table.

SHOWTIME!

❶ Show the fan of jacks and explain to your friends that the four jacks are thieves. Make up any story you like about them robbing the bank. Use your imagination!

❷ Close the fan, being careful not to expose the three extra cards. Place this pile on top of the deck face down. When you put the cards face down, the three extra cards will now be on top, followed by the four jacks.

❸ While you explain to the audience that the jacks are hiding from the police, remove the first top card and bury it into the deck, keeping it face down the entire time. You call this the first jack (it is really the first extra card that goes into the deck).

❹ Repeat this twice more, burying the other two extra cards in the deck, all the while telling your story about the jacks.

❺ Now turn the next top card face up and place it onto the deck. You call this the fourth jack (even though it is actually the first). All four jacks are sitting at the top of the deck now. Tell your friends that with a finger snap, you will bring the four jacks together. Snap your fingers and slowly turn the cards over to reveal the first three jacks are once again on top of the deck. If audience members want to examine the deck, have them do so at this time.

PEPPERY
PRESTIDIGITATION

You show your friends a bowl of water and sprinkle pepper into it, covering the surface. Invite your friend to dip his or her finger into the water. The pepper clings to his or her finger, but when you put your finger into the bowl—the pepper quickly floats away from your finger!

WHAT YOU'LL NEED
• **bar of soap** • **bowl of water** • **pepper**

GETTING READY

Before the trick begins, secretly coat your index finger with a light layer of soap from the soap bar. Wipe off any excess and let it dry. It should dry clear.

SHOWTIME

❶ Show your friends the bowl of water and sprinkle a generous amount of pepper into the bowl. The pepper will float on the surface of the water.

❷ Invite your friend to dip his or her index finger into the water and pepper. Your friend will be left with wet pepper on his or her finger.

❸ Sprinkle more pepper into the bowl, if needed, so that it covers the surface once again. Now dip your soap-coated finger into the water. The pepper will move away from your finger toward the rim of the bowl! It will look very magical.